LITTLE BIG BOOK

S0-EAR-871

EARLY AIRCRAFT

MARK HEWISH

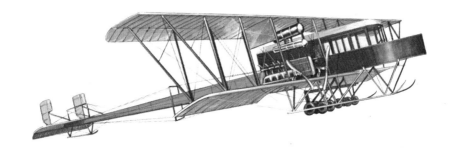

Editor: Trisha Pike   Designer: Jacky Cowdrey
Picture Researcher: Anne-Marie Ehrlich

Purnell

Above: Daedalus and Icarus flew across the sea but Icarus drowned.

1 THE DREAM OF FLIGHT

Men have flown to the Moon and back again. Air passengers can now fly at twice the speed of sound (1,087 feet per second). But it is only about 75 years since the first airplane flew successfully.

Men have always wanted to fly like the birds. Many thousands of years ago Daedalus and his son Icarus flew by making wings of

Right: The Malmesbury monk broke all his bones when he landed.

feathers. But that was only a make-believe story. The first real flyers went up into the air in a balloon. The Montgolfier brothers filled the balloon with hot air.

Men such as Sir George Cayley and Otto Lilienthal made gliders. Then the Wright brothers made the first flight in a real airplane in December, 1903.

By the end of the First World War in 1918 airplanes were flying at a speed of 150 m.p.h. Soon there were planes for carrying passengers.

Below: Leonardo da Vinci made a drawing of a flapping machine.

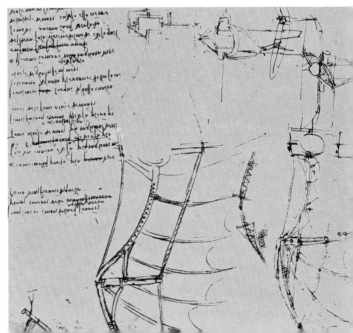

2 BEFORE THE WRIGHTS

The first people to fly were two Frenchmen, in 1783. They drifted through the sky over Paris in a Montgolfier balloon filled with hot air. Many people tried to copy the birds by fitting wings to their arms and flapping them. They did not fly because the muscles in a man's chest and shoulders are simply not strong enough.

Sir George Cayley had a better idea. He built gliders which could carry a pilot. Then men tried to drive the gliders with steam engines. But the steam engines were much too heavy. The planes could not take off. So Otto Lilienthal worked out how to make the best wing shapes by building big gliders. He built a

Below: Two Frenchmen made the first balloon flight.

Above: Cyrano de Bergerac thought he could fly by wearing bottles of dew or smoke.

number of gliders. He thought of fitting a small engine to one of them but died before he could test it.

The Wright brothers decided to try a gasoline engine. There was not one that was light enough. So they invented a really light engine.

When they fitted this engine to a glider they were able to fly.

Above: Otto Lilienthal flying one of his gliders. He made over 2,000 test flights.

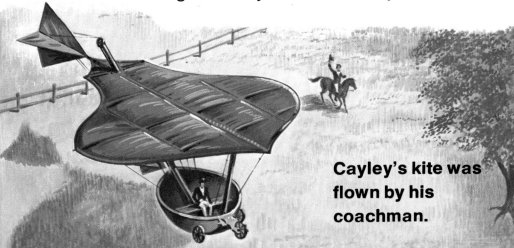

Cayley's kite was flown by his coachman.

3 THE WRIGHT BROTHERS

Wilbur Wright.

Orville Wright.

The first men to fly in an airplane driven by an engine were Orville and Wilbur Wright.

The Wright brothers began by building gliders. They wanted the best possible glider. So they made hundreds of tests with different models in a wind tunnel only 6 feet long.

Then they built a machine called the Flyer. They built a special light gasoline engine for it.

Orville made the world's first real powered flight on December 17, 1903. He lay on the lower wing of the Flyer and started the engine. The machine began to move forward.

Above: The Wright brothers made the first powered flight with Flyer I. It was in the air for twelve seconds. The same day they flew again.

Wilbur kept the plane steady. Suddenly the Flyer lifted off its wooden rail and Orville was flying.

In 1908 Wilbur took the first two-seater aircraft to France. He was able to carry passengers.

He showed that flying was really possible. Until then many people still thought that the Wrights were making up their stories about flying.

Left: At first people did not believe the Wright brothers could fly but soon many visitors came to France to watch them.

4 AIR RACES

Right: Many people came to watch the first air races.

Soon people wanted to find out who was best at flying. So they held air races. Wealthy people, companies and newspapers offered trophies and prizes of money. Some of the prizes were very big.

In 1909 the *Daily Mail* offered a prize of £1,000 for the first British pilot to fly one mile in a British aircraft. The American Sam Cody became a British subject so that he could take part in the race. But he had an accident before the start and J. T. C. Moore-Brabazon won the race.

In 1910, a Frenchman, Louis Paulhan, won £10,000, offered by the *Daily Mail* newspaper. He did this by beating Claude Grahame-White in

Right: Sam Cody made the first airplane flight in Britain in 1908.

Above: The first pilot's license was issued to J. T. C. Moore-Brabazon.

the London-to-Manchester race.
Airplane engines often broke down, and pilots had to do very daring things to stay in the race. With the prize money they could pay for better planes. So air races really helped to build better planes. They encouraged pilots to try new things.

Above: Louis Blériot lands at Dover.

5   THE AMAZING BLÉRIOT

Louis Blériot was the first person to fly from one country to another. He flew his Type XI across the English Channel in 1909. He won the *Daily Mail*'s £1,000 prize, but had a lot of luck. His engine overheated while he was over the water, and a shower of rain cooled it down just in time.

Blériot thought that monoplanes were best. These planes have only one wing on each side. Biplanes, such as the Flyers, have two sets of wings, one above the other. Nowadays almost all aircraft are monoplanes.

Above: Blériot XI, the first to fly the Channel.

Above: Blériot's first completely successful plane.

Blériot's monoplanes were very successful. Lieutenant Jean Conneau won his races with a Blériot machine. So did Claude Grahame-White.

Blériot wanted more people to share the pleasure of flying. In 1909 his Type XII was the first plane to carry two passengers. Two years later a Blériot Airbus flew three miles with eleven passengers.

Frenchman Louis Blériot was an early pilot.

Below: After Blériot's crossing there were many flying shows.

6 SEAPLANES AND FLYING BOATS

Calm water is almost flat, and so it makes a very good surface for taking off and landing. Several types of aircraft can be used. Floatplanes, also called seaplanes, have floats under the wings or fuselage (the plane's body). Flying boats rest in the water on a hull like that of a boat. Amphibians can take off from water or land.

The first seaplane was Henri Fabre's Hydravion of 1910. It

Above: The first seaplane to fly was Fabre's.

Above: Glen Curtiss flew the first really practical seaplane in 1911.

Below: The Felixstowe F.2A flying boat.

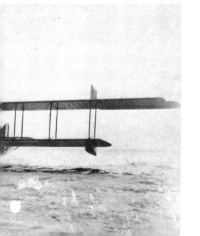

worked, but not very well. Glen Curtiss made the first really successful flight in 1911. His plane was a Golden Flyer. It had a float under the plane's body and two smaller floats under the lower wings.

Later, Curtiss planes had twin floats. He also built amphibians with wheels as well as floats. Seaplanes were used in war too. During the First World War they were launched from both ships and the land. Big flying boats also bombed ships and submarines.

One of the most famous flying competitions was for seaplanes. It was called the Schneider Trophy, which began in 1913. This race was held for nearly 20 years.

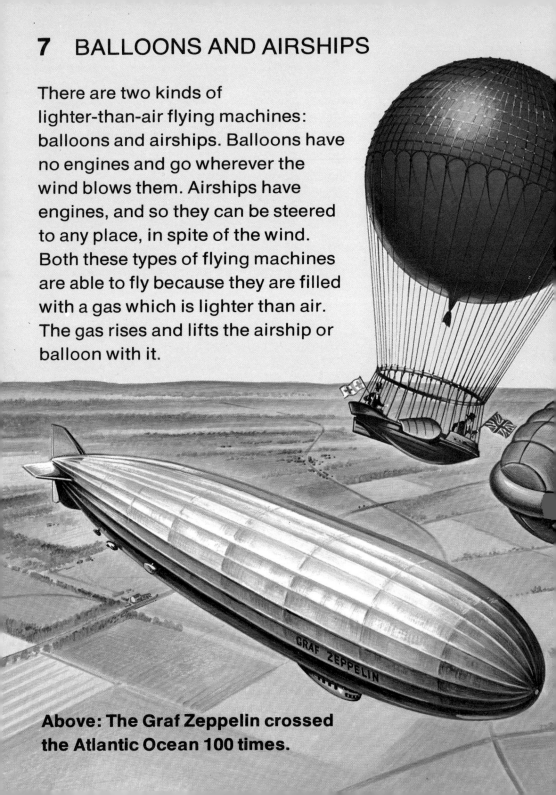

7 BALLOONS AND AIRSHIPS

There are two kinds of lighter-than-air flying machines: balloons and airships. Balloons have no engines and go wherever the wind blows them. Airships have engines, and so they can be steered to any place, in spite of the wind. Both these types of flying machines are able to fly because they are filled with a gas which is lighter than air. The gas rises and lifts the airship or balloon with it.

Above: The Graf Zeppelin crossed the Atlantic Ocean 100 times.

Left: The Channel was first crossed by air in 1785.

Above: The first airship to be filled with helium. Helium is safer than hydrogen as it does not burn.

Below: Balloons were used to spot the enemy.

This gas is hot air, hydrogen or helium. Hydrogen can lift heavier weights, but it burns easily and so is dangerous. Helium does not burn, but it is expensive to make.

The first flight with a hydrogen balloon was made in 1783. This was just after the first trip in a hot-air balloon. In 1785 the English Channel was crossed by air for the first time.

The most famous airship builder was Count Ferdinand von Zeppelin. He started in 1900. Twelve years later airships called Zeppelins were carrying many passengers between German cities.

Balloons were also used in the First World War. The first heavy bombers were airships.

8 BETTER LUCK NEXT TIME

One man was very disappointed when the Wright brothers made their first real flight in 1903. His name was Samuel Langley. He thought that the glory was going to be his. He tested his flying machine a few days before. The Airdrome, as it was called, took off from a boat in the Potomac River near Washington. But instead of flying, it hit a post and plunged into the water.

Many other people built flying machines which did not fly. In France, Trajan Vuia made three

Below: Langley's Airdrome was a flop.

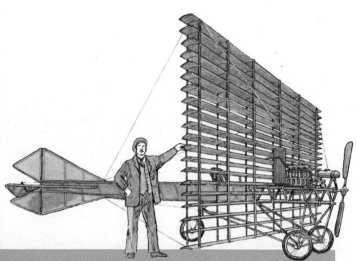

This plane had so many wings it looked like a Venetian blind.

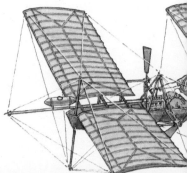

machines in 1906 and 1907. The longest flight of all three covered only 26 yards.

Sam Cody, an American working in England, did better with his Army Airplane No 1. At least it flew, although changes were made to it after almost every trip.

Some of the most interesting flops were made by Horatio Phillips. He had thought of many good ideas to help make better aircraft. But, unfortunately, he could not make his own planes work properly.

His planes had long, narrow wings one on top of the other, so that they looked like a Venetian blind.

Above: A plane based on a Phillips' multiplane.

Above: Sam Cody did manage to get his British Army Airplane No. 1 to fly.

9 ALL AT SEA

Early aircraft took off and landed slowly, so they only needed a short runway. There was plenty of space on big warships. Soon planes were being used to spot enemy ships.

The first takeoff from a ship was made in 1910. On November 14, Eugene Ely, in a Curtiss biplane, took off from a wooden platform above the deck of a light cruiser. The underside of the plane hit the water, but he just managed to keep flying. Two months later Ely made the first landing on a ship at sea in a similar kind of biplane.

In 1912 Commander Samson of

Below: The first successful landing on a ship.

Above: Eugene Ely was the first pilot to take off and land on a ship.

Above: Commander Samson takes off.

the Royal Navy took off from a battleship while it was moving. The plane took off from specially built ramps that covered up a gun turret.

The Royal Navy built aircraft carriers. Planes could then take off from a flat deck. In 1917, a Sopwith Pup biplane tried to land on a ship. But the plane ran off the deck and the pilot drowned.

Later aircraft carriers had flight decks for the whole length of the ship. Planes could then take off and land easily.

10 SIKORSKY THINKS BIG

Igor Sikorsky is often called "the father of the helicopter". He invented and built the first helicopters that worked. However, before he invented these machines he built the world's first big aircraft.

It was called Le Grand, which means the Great One in French. Sikorsky built and flew it in Russia. Le Grand had four engines and its wings measured more than 30 yards from tip to tip. The passengers sat in a big cabin with glass sides. They could walk around and look over the side.

Early in the next year, 1914,

Above: Igor Sikorsky.

Below: Le Grand had four engines.

Left: Le Grand's passengers sat in a big cabin with glass sides.

Sikorsky built an even bigger plane. It was called the Ilya Mourometz. The wings of this plane measured nearly 32 yards from tip to tip. At the back of the plane's body there were places for the passengers to eat and sleep.

When the First World War started, Russia used many Ilya Mourometzes as bombers. All together they were called the Squadron of Flying Ships. The later ones could carry over 1500 pounds of bombs.

Above: The Czar used Ilya Mourometzes.

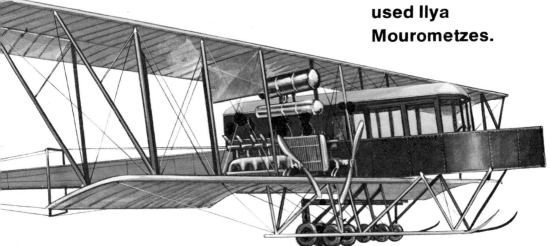

11 AIRCRAFT GO TO WAR

Even before the First World War started, people were thinking of ways of fighting with planes. Planes could move around with much greater speed and freedom than balloons and airships. So planes were used for spying on the enemy.

Aircraft could also drop bombs. This was tried by the Italians in 1911. The bombs were carried in the cockpit and dropped over the side by the pilot or observer (the man who watches out for the enemy).

Guns were made to shoot down aircraft. But the best way to shoot down an enemy plane was with

Below: The first bombs were dropped over the aircraft's side.

Above: A machine gun fitted to a Grahame-White biplane.

Above: Two D.H.2s escort an observation plane.

another aircraft. At first the crew (the pilot and the observer) fired rifles and pistols at the enemy. Then machine guns were fitted to the planes. These guns could fire faster, and they could hit the targets better. There were air battles between planes called "dog fights".

Observers were very busy men. They had to help the pilot find his way. They also noted down interesting details to help the army.

Above: Manfred von Richthofen, "The Red Baron."

Below: A German Fokker D.R.1 triplane turns from the enemy.

In early two-seater planes it was the observer who aimed the gun. But in one-seater planes the pilot did it. This was difficult, because he had to fly the plane at the same time.

The pilot could only do both jobs properly if the gun was fitted just in front of him. He could then look through the gun sights and steer the plane to point the gun at the target.

But many one-seater planes had the engine and propeller at the front, between the gun and its target. Wooden propellers broke if a bullet

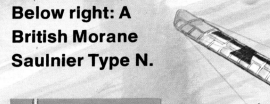

Propellers were protected by steel plates.

Left: The pilot of this British F.2A fighter machine guns the sky.

hit them. So steel plates were fitted on the propeller blades. Bullets from the plane's gun bounced off these plates without harming them.

Pilots in Germany used a different method. Their planes were fitted with a special machine. It stopped the gun from firing when a propeller blade was in the way. This machine was called interrupter gear, because it interrupted, or stopped, the stream of bullets. The first planes fitted with interrupter gear were Fokker monoplanes.

13 BIG BOMBERS

Below: A Caproni CA.41 triplane.

When the First World War started, most warplanes were small and could not carry heavy loads. The biggest bombs which they dropped weighed only 22 lbs. each. But the Ilya Mourometz was flying in Russia, and this showed that big bombers were possible.

Early in the war, France used

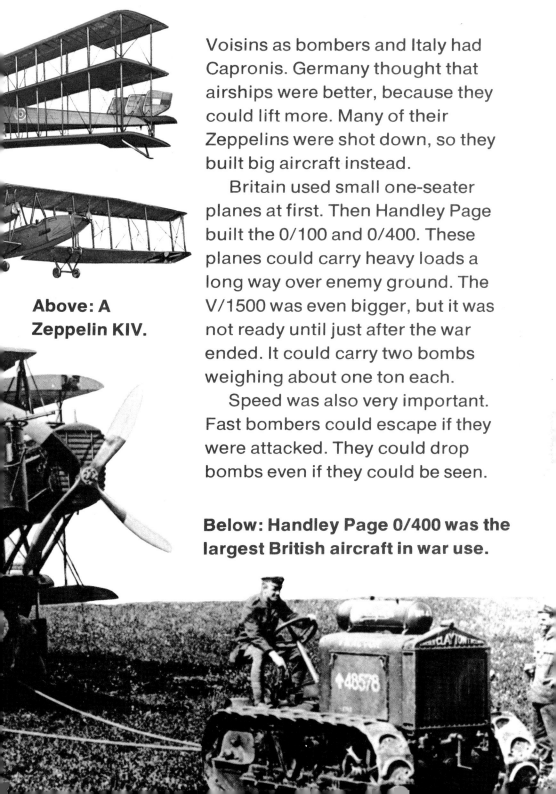

Voisins as bombers and Italy had Capronis. Germany thought that airships were better, because they could lift more. Many of their Zeppelins were shot down, so they built big aircraft instead.

Britain used small one-seater planes at first. Then Handley Page built the 0/100 and 0/400. These planes could carry heavy loads a long way over enemy ground. The V/1500 was even bigger, but it was not ready until just after the war ended. It could carry two bombs weighing about one ton each.

Speed was also very important. Fast bombers could escape if they were attacked. They could drop bombs even if they could be seen.

Above: A Zeppelin KIV.

Below: Handley Page 0/400 was the largest British aircraft in war use.

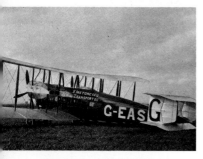

**Above: Fokker
F.II four-seater.**

**Above: A Vickers
Vimy Commercial.**

At the end of the First World War there were many bombers which were not needed any more. Some of these were turned into airliners by fitting seats for passengers. The first flight from one country to another with fare-paying passengers was started in August 1919. The flight was from London to Paris, and the plane was a converted D.H.4 single-engine bomber.

Soon bigger and more comfortable planes were built. A new body with room for ten

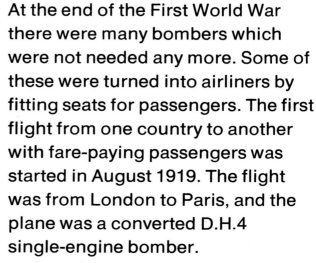

passengers was fitted to the Vickers Vimy bomber. In France, the Farman Goliath carried up to twelve people on journeys from Paris to London and Brussels.

Germany started carrying passengers in Zeppelins before the war. The Germans also built airliners for passengers. The Fokker F.II, with room for four passengers, was later built in Holland. Junkers built the J.13, the first airliner to be made of metal only.

The first regular passenger air service in America was started in 1914 but did not last for long.

Below: Passengers flying in the D.H.9 had to be dressed up warmly against the cold.

The first regular passenger air service flew from Hounslow airport in 1919.

15 EARLY HELICOPTERS

Helicopters do not have wings like other aircraft. Instead, they have a very large propeller on top. It is called a rotor. The rotor keeps the helicopter in the air. It is turned by the engine.

The first helicopter to lift a man off the ground was the Breguet-Richet Gyroplane No. 1 in 1907. However, it had no steering and it rose only five feet into the air. Also in 1907 a helicopter built by another Frenchman, Paul Cornu, stayed still just above the ground for about 20 seconds on its first flight.

Above: Leonardo was an artist and a scientist.

Above: He made this drawing but it was never built.

Above: Igor Sikorsky's VS-300.

Above: Modern helicopters look very similar to some of the first helicopters.

Below: Cornu's helicopter was the first to be piloted.

These early helicopters could not do very much. The engines were not powerful enough. These machines were also difficult to control.

The first helicopter that really worked did not fly until 1940. This machine was Igor Sikorsky's VS-300. But in 1911 another Russian, Boris Yariev, built a machine with a rotor on the tail as well as on top. This was to stop the helicopter itself going around when the big rotor overhead turned very fast. Most modern helicopters still have a small rotor on their tail.

WORDS YOU MAY NOT KNOW

Bomber   An aircraft used for dropping bombs.

Cockpit   The space where the pilot sits in an aircraft.

Competition   A contest between two or more people to decide who is best at something.

Cruiser   A warship fitted with large guns.

Enemy   Someone who is against another person.

Gun turret   A rounded shelter which holds guns and gunners usually found on warplanes.

Machine gun   An automatic gun that fires a stream of bullets.

Passenger   A person who travels in vehicles such as a plane, ship or a bus.

Propeller   A plane part that slices through the air and pulls the plane forward, in the same way that a screw cuts into wood.

Propeller blade   The flat part of a propeller.

Ramp   A slope.

Runway   A special surface for aircraft to take off from and land on.

Weapon   A tool which is used to hurt or damage someone or something.